HE CHEATED!

SO, WHAT NOW?

Emerging from the pain of infidelity

better and not bitter

Angela Williams

HE CHEATED! SO, WHAT NOW?

Emerging from the pain of infidelity better and not bitter

Copyright © 2022 Angela Williams

All rights reserved.

No part of this publication may be reproduced, distributed, or transmitted in any form or by any means, including photocopying, recording, or other electronic or mechanical methods, without the prior written permission of the publisher, except in the case of brief quotations embodied in critical reviews and certain other noncommercial uses permitted by copyright law.

Dedication

This book is dedicated to my husband. Jeff my love, my appreciation, respect, and commitment to you is deeper than anything I can express on these pages. Although your actions were the source of my torture, your tenacity, understanding and love for me helped to bring me back into the light. If there was ever a man to make recompense for his mistakes, you are the one. You never judged or made me feel like my actions or my feelings were too much or uncalled for. Even as I threatened your very life, you tolerated every phase of my recovery with the grace and the strength of a king. I love the way you love me.

To my daughter, Jayla. You are one of the most interesting human beings I have ever met. Your wisdom and wit are nothing short of amazing. Watching you become your own woman is like witnessing a beautiful butterfly slowly, yet anxiously, emerging from its cocoon.

You are gorgeous inside and out; don't you ever forget it.

I pray that you always love yourself as much as God loves you.

It is an honor to be your mother and to have a seat on the front row of your life.

Come what may. Always be good to yourself.

To my handsome, powerful sons, LeRoy, Jewon, and Jerrell, your presence is magical. Through the darkest times for our family, you have prevailed.

I have had the privilege of seeing you transition from boys to good and honorable gentlemen. I love you so much. Keep getting up and continue to enjoy your journey.

Momma

Preface

I had been married for more than 16 years when I found out that I had been deceived by the person I trusted and depended on more than anyone else on earth. I learned that my husband, my boo thang, my love, had cheated on me. And that's not all. He had fathered a baby to boot. The state of bewilderment and confusion almost killed me.

This revelation slung me into a six-year tailspin. I felt as if I had been punched in the throat. Sometimes I thought I was losing my mind. To be honest, for a while, I was so close to the edge that a deep whisper could have blown me miles away.

I couldn't see. I couldn't think. I couldn't even breathe.

Unfortunately, my story is not unique. I'm not the first wife to be cheated on, and I will not be the last. Women from all walks of life experience pain caused by a partner's infidelity. And so many live and die sad, miserable, and bitter. I refused to do that.

"He Cheated! So What Now" is a story about my journey from bitter to better. There is no formula for dealing with a situation like this. I hope that my journey and the tips and tools that I share in this short book will help you to overcome the hurt in far less time than it took me. Remember, this is your journey. Do what works for you. My intent here is to offer suggestions as I share what worked for me. So as my pastor Michael Moore says: "Eat the meat and spit out the bones."

Contents

Dedication ii

Preface iv

Introduction viii

Phase #1: Shock and Circumstances 1

    The Shame of it All 7

Phase 2: How Numb Can You Be? 9

Phase 3: Hurt 16

Phase 4: Mad as Hell 21

Phase 5: I Don't Give a Damn! 26

The Red Tag Syndrome 35

The Recovery, Restoration, and Discovery 39

    Recovery 41

    Decide 43

    Restoration 44

    Forgive Him 45

Forgive Yourself 46

Discovery 47

Do Something Just for You 49

Take Your Time, Sis 51

Keep Your Tribe Small 53

Be Quiet 54

Speak On It! 55

Putting In the Work 56

Journaling 56

Self-Care Is Not Selfishness. It Is a Must!................. 57

The Epilogue 60

About Angela Williams 66

Introduction

To say I survived this betrayal is an understatement. I thrived because of it. I came out of it a better person, happier, and more fulfilled than I had ever been in my adult life. My momma used to say that struggle will draw you or drive you. That statement means that when life throws you a gut punch, you have two choices: You can stay down (the draw) or get up (the drive). I decided to get up, put my dukes up, and fight. I didn't want to be angry and miserable for the rest of my life or that chick who spends her days spilling everybody else's tea and complaining about the most minute things. You know her. She is the chick that walks in the room with the *something stinks* look on her face most of the time.

I intend to help and inspire other women experiencing pain due to cheating and betrayal to recover and discover their own personal power and value. I pray that you understand this truth: You don't have to be bitter. You can be whole and happy. Furthermore, you deserve to be whole, happy, and to enjoy your journey...for real!

Full disclosure -- I chose to stay in my marriage, but don't get it twisted. This book is not a Tammy Wynette "Stand By Your Man" kind of groove. This conversation is not about how to save your marriage or how to forgive him and fall in love again. This book is not about the kids, the in-laws, the finances, the rent, the image, or any of those common reasons. This is all about you choosing to recover and live your best life.

This book is about learning to breathe again.

Phase #1: Shock and Circumstances

Shock: the act of being surprised or upset because something unexpected, unusual, or unpleasant has happened.

Back in the day, the elders used the term "outdone" to express a sense of disbelief. If you have ever witnessed someone in shock, you know one of the key characteristics of this state is silence. We all understand that people are unique and react differently to trauma. No one knows how they will react until faced with the situation. Some people go straight into rage, but shocked silence is a common reaction when trying to make sense of unthinkable nonsense.

Shock and disbelief were my initial reactions. My man cheating on me was such an absurd notion that I literally burst into laughter. So, here is how it all went down...

The year before this revelation came to light, our home had been heavily damaged in a fire. It was uninhabitable, and we had to temporarily relocate. We had just returned home from an eight-month extended stay hotel apartment when the call came in. This one phone call changed my world and everything in it. I found out the extent of my husband's infidelity.

He was a truck driver for over twenty-five years, so being away three-to-four nights a week was common for us. But at some point, I noticed a change in him. I couldn't put my finger on it, but what I knew for sure was that we were not getting along, and he was different.

Hold up! Before you go there, I make no excuses for his behavior. He is a grown-ass man and that cross is his and his alone to bear. I am simply providing context. However, I never thought in a million years that my husband would be unfaithful to me.

As a child coming of age in the 60s, 70s, and 80s, discipline meant a whipping. In my momma's house, there were very little rules to this exercise. You got hit on whatever spot so happened to be exposed. The surprise licks or the ones you didn't see coming were the worst. It stunned and hurt so badly that it caused a phenomenon we playfully referred to as *the silent cry*. If you are not familiar with it, let me help you out.

Immediately after the lick occurs, your mouth opens to cry but nothing comes out. There is complete silence. The SILENCE is then followed by a deep breath and an alarming scream. It's the shock of it all coupled with the subsequent pain that causes this reaction. This is the best way I know to describe what I felt at the time. The pain was so severe, I couldn't even cry.

Eventually, all I could do was scream.

Several months before returning home, an incident occurred that indicated that he had been out here "in these streets" living fowl. I could not prove an offense, but from what I did know, it was obvious to me that he had not been on his best behavior. Eventually, he had to tell me something. Initially, he came to me with a corny, *it wasn't me* type of excuse. Then he broke out the famous, "Baby, it was just a one-time fable." I didn't buy it when he said it then. However, I was distracted and didn't care enough to get my Jessica Fletcher/CSI on and launch a full-scale investigation. Either way, I let it go.

We were still on rocky ground when we moved back to the house, but I was feeling pretty good about moving forward. New Years is my favorite holiday. It always feels like a fresh start to me. So, with that, I felt hopeful. With a good-as-new house and a fresh start, I was thinking that we would put this behind us and move forward. I remember thinking, *we are going to be alright.*

Ah…hahaha, sike!!

One day, the phone rang. I noticed that he took the call into another room, but the kids and I were laughing and talking loudly, so I didn't think much of it. After a while, I could see he plopped down on an ottoman we kept in a corner of our bedroom. He was holding his head in his hands. From a distance, I could tell something was wrong. When he returned to the kitchen with us, there was a look of sheer terror on the man's face. I realized it must have been something serious, but I half-heartedly tried to maintain the good vibes we had created.

I playfully snapped, "What's wrong with you?"

Again, he gave me a look as if somebody had died.

He grabbed my hand and asked me to come to the bedroom with him. This man looked me squarely in the eyes and said, "That was that girl telling me that she has an 18-month-old baby, and it is mine."

This has got to be a prank!

I instantly burst into laughter, "EX…CUSE ME, say what? Boy, please."

I thought it was the most absurd thing I had ever heard.

But this was not The Steve Harvey Morning Radio Show, and this was not Nephew Tommy, and this was not a prank. And although it made absolutely no sense to me, this was real.

Confused doesn't begin to explain my state of mind. It took me a while to digest what I was hearing. At that point, I wasn't even angry. I was neck-deep in denial, but I knew my life would never be the same.

I couldn't breathe. It was like somebody had sucker-punched me in the throat. I couldn't think. My brain stopped processing anything, anything at all. I couldn't swallow. The lumps in my throat made sure of that. All I wanted to do was catch my breath and I couldn't even do that! I felt like I was suffocating from the inside out. My whole world was crashing around me and all I wanted was to take a deep breath.

I demanded, "Call her back. NOW!!" There was no need to introduce myself. I just started in with the number one question: "How do you know that this child belongs to my husband?"

Her response was even more pathetic than I had expected. This girl said, "I have had two other blood tests that were negative, so he has to be the daddy."

"Say what now?"

So not only did she have an affair with my husband, but she didn't even know who the baby's daddy was. In my mind, not only did *he have an affair*, but, in my opinion, he didn't even bother to upgrade.

I was outdone. The thought of him intimately touching someone else and someone else touching him shrank next to the idea that he had an emotional connection with a woman who had been so lax in her sexual encounters that she had to perform three DNA tests to determine who the child's father was disgusted me.

So now we waited for the results of a blood test.

I didn't cuss or scream and punch him in his face. I didn't hit him over the head with a hot cast iron skillet full of Crisco oil. I didn't do anything. I was in shock, and I didn't tell a soul.

What was I going to say? I think my husband got a baby by a girl who doesn't know who her baby daddy is? I needed to have proof. I needed to know for sure.

The Shame of it All

It was two years before I shared anything with anybody. Now looking back, it was probably one of the wisest moves I made during this period. Had I told my loved ones and friends about the situation, they would've shared strong opinions and never-ending advice. Their passionate responses would have given me more BS to deal with, and I couldn't handle that. So rather than taking the risk of dumping out my frustrations on other people, I didn't say a word. I kept remembering the wisdom shared with me on my wedding day.

When we got married in 1991, we were members of a small church of about thirty members. Everybody in the church was in attendance. As the minister asked, "Does anyone have a reason why these two people should not be joined together in holy matrimony?" Everyone did the common looking around. That's when the mother of the church stood up.

"I ain't got no reason why these two young folks should not be joined in marriage." Then, with a pointed finger, Ms. Hattie sternly admonished, "Baby let me tell you something. Don't you ever let nobody tell you nothin' about yo husband. Whatever go on between you and him, let it stay between you and him."

I had built my entire married life on that philosophy. But it wasn't just between him and me anymore. He had brought two more people into our lives without my knowledge or consent. He had betrayed my trust. To be honest, the real reason I kept the news to myself is because I was too embarrassed.

How was he going to cheat on me? I had been good to him, and I'm smart. I may not look like the cover of a magazine but I'm cute, I'm resourceful, and I'm sexy. I'm a good Christian wife and mother. Hell, I'm a badd chick! So, what did he see in this other woman that would make him put everything on the line? Was there something wrong with me? What was it about her that would make him risk it all?

I didn't have the answer to any of these questions. Truth be told, to this day, I still don't have the answers. But I am confident that whatever the reason had absolutely nothing to do with me.

Phase 2: How numb can you be?

Numb: Unable to think, feel, or respond normally.

Some medical procedures require the use of a numbing agent, like anesthesia. Upon discharge, the attendant will warn against doing anything that involves the affected area. These warnings are issued because you risk causing injury or damage that will only be felt when life returns to the area. The numbness is dangerous because it is nearly impossible to feel the impact on the affected area until it is too late.

The catatonic state of shock is debilitating. My four children, three boys and one girl, ranging in ages 6 to 20, needed me. However, at the time, I was a bare minimum mother. Emotionally unavailable, I could only provide shelter, schooling, food, and clothing. They, like me, were the least deserving of the pain and confusion that had infiltrated our family. Along with the regular challenges of growing up, they were also trying to process what was happening at home. Chaos, anger, and distrust were tearing our family to pieces, and I was too weak and disconnected to offer them any meaningful help. My emotional numbness lasted for what seemed like forever.

It is here that I ceased to feel.

It is here that I ceased to care.

It is here that I stopped breathing.

I was suffocating and no one cared, not even me. In this catatonic state, nothing mattered, not even the thoughts that ruminated around in my mind all day every day.

I had checked out from everything and everybody. Contrary to the external silence that accompanies the catatonic state, this stage is traumatic, internally noisy, and can be the most damaging. I walked around in what seemed like a perpetual daze. What I heard most of the time was the w*a-wa-wa* sound that Charlie Brown heard when his teacher spoke. I heard people talking out loud but saying nothing. This may sound overly dramatic to some, but my response to that train of thought is, "keep on living."

Where was I? I digressed for a moment. Now, let's get back to my children...

Unfortunately, I was operating on fumes. I had turned inward, and I didn't see the signs of distress in my children. I had coined a phrase, "I have my own bag of tricks." This meant I only had the time and energy for self-preservation and to meet their basic needs. Imagine the damage that one statement caused to young boys who were experiencing pivotal moments on a near-daily basis.

One of my sons was being bullied in school and I nearly missed it. By the time I realized that he was in trouble, it was almost too late. Up until this point he was a jovial, lighthearted, friendly child or so I thought. One morning while leaving to drop the boys off at school, I noticed that he had about thirty to forty extremely sharpened pencils tightly wound together by several rubber bands. When I saw it, I asked him why he had this contraption.

With tears in his eyes he responded, "If somebody touch me today, I'm gonna kill em."

Of course, I swung into action. I demanded meetings and an immediate resolution. The next school year, we withdrew him from that school environment. I am grateful to God that he is now a well-adjusted, independent man.

Several months later, the test results were in. As I read the results, the lump in my throat got even worse. In a fashion not half as dramatic as a Maury Povich, the test confirmed that my husband of 16 years was the father of another woman's baby.

Amidst all of this, we needed to go to court to determine child support. The day of the court hearing was hectic for everybody,

I'm sure, but I'm talking about me right now. As we waited to be called before the family court judge, I scanned the room looking for a sign that would indicate which one of these witches had been with my husband. Sitting in the waiting room with several other people, I realized that I wouldn't know her from a can of paint.

I asked my husband, "Do not let this woman walk up on me and I not know who she is!"

My mind was in turmoil. Which one of these thots had kissed him, rubbed his back, or fixed him a plate? Who in here went half on a baby with my man?

When it was time for the involved parties to go into the courtroom, the bailiff stopped me in my tracks.

"Ma'am, who are you?"

I responded, "I am his wife, Mrs. Williams."

Without any reservations, this man looked me eyeball to eyeball and said, "You cannot come in. Only the parents of the child are allowed in the courtroom."

The image of the court bailiff, a husky cocoa-skinned man in a tan and brown law enforcement uniform pointing towards the exit lived in my head rent-free for a long time. At the time I thought it was so unfair. The man was doing his job. He was enforcing the policy set forth by Jefferson County, Alabama.

I was livid and could not accept his directive. "What?! What do you mean? I have been married to this man for 18 years. Whatever happens in that room affects me and my children just like it affects him, her, and her child."

"I understand ma'am." And as he pointed towards the door, he said, "It doesn't matter, you can't come in."

Next to learning that my husband cheated, that was one of the most humiliating experiences I have ever had in my life. What I heard was *I don't matter*. My 18 years of commitment and sacrifice **didn't matter**.

I felt so weak, my legs almost gave way underneath me. It took every ounce of strength I could muster just to stand upright. With a lump in my throat as big as a baseball, I held my head up and slowly exited the building without breaking down. I imagined people in the waiting room staring at me whispering. I also imagined them saying, "She gone cry when she gets in the car."

Looking back, it was probably best for all parties involved. Can you imagine the series of courtroom explosions five days a week? The snot slinging and fist swinging would've been nonstop.

After two years of utter disbelief, a blood test, a visit to family court and a judge's order for child support confirmed paternity of this child, it forced me to face reality. My husband had fathered a child with another woman. Our silo had been breached. All the plans we had made for the future of our family were no more.

Everything I thought to be my truth and my reality was only a vapor, a figment of my imagination, and there was absolutely nothing I could do about it. I felt as if someone close to me had died. I was exhausted, helpless and scared, but I couldn't articulate what I was feeling.

Now I realize that I was in mourning.

Life was happening all around me. The seasons were changing, the sun continued to rise, people were carrying on with life and I barely noticed. I was in the room but for all intents and purposes, I was just occupying space.

When I was about 5 or 6 years old, I nearly cut off my right pointer finger on a broken Coca-Cola bottle. To this day, that finger is still numb. It's still attached to my hand, but it's numb. I can use it, but there is no feeling in it. I polish the nail on it and even place nice jewelry on it. It looks good, yet it is still void of feeling. Just like my pointy finger, I was NUMB. I presented a good front though.

I still went to church, lifted holy hands, and even continued to teach bible classes.

Some women have been in this state of mind for years. They are on the scene but not present in the moment. Some of us allow hurt, anger, and bitterness to rule our lives. We have made a pact and formed a bond with these negative emotions. Some of us will hold on to bitterness, hurt, and anger with everything we have. We protect and nurture it and dare anybody to question it. Because of someone else's actions, we have decided to never be happy and whole again.

We are taking in air but not breathing. We exist, but living is a foreign concept.

I sometimes wonder about the opportunities I missed during this time. Not being present in the moment will cost us mental health, emotional strength, financial stability, and fulfilling relationships.

Come back to the light. Bitterness costs too much.

"Happiness is a journey, not a destination."

Alfred D. Souza

Phase 3: Hurt

Hurt: Distressed or offended by another person's behavior.

It doesn't matter if it is mental or physical. When pain is present, it takes the spotlight. **Nothing else matters**. We will do just about anything to stop it. Commercials that advertise medicines are interesting to me. There is always a voice-over attached warning that although this medication will cure or treat your condition if taken, it runs the risk of causing damage elsewhere in the body. Sometimes these side effects are even more damaging than the original condition.

"But I just want the pain to stop," you say. Slow down and take the time to determine the right approach for you. Remember some decisions are irreversible.

"Hurt" is the opposite of "Numb." Upon emerging out of that catatonic-like state, this next phase I entered had me sensitive to the core. I felt everything, magnified by a thousand. It had crept in like smoke from fresh embers and caught me by surprise.

I call this the **hump phase** because it served as a tipping point or a crossroad. It is here that I would face my situation head-on. It is here that I would accept the truth. Contrary to the zombie-like state from which I was emerging, hurt allowed me to feel again. I still couldn't breathe, but at least I was conscious.

The courthouse experience had shaken me to my core. It snatched me out of my catatonic state and slammed me head-first into a fit of rage. After that courthouse debacle, I sat in the parking lot revving up the motor in my car. I had made up my mind. *I'm going to run over both of them as soon as they come out of that building* ...PERIOD. That is as far as I could go in my thinking. The consequences were a non-factor.

I remember seeing her, and it planted a negative yet vivid visual inside my mind. I can still see what she had on. She wasn't even *all that*! Through fits of tears, heaving, laughter, and screams, my thoughts vacillated from one irrational thought to the next. *That MF better not walk out with that B. What was he thinking? Was that what he risked everything for? REALLY? He done "F'd up. Imma kill them MF's. Oh yeah, they got the right one!*

Suddenly, my phone rang. It was my oldest son's father. We were good friends by then, which is very strange considering he was also my abuser -- the details of that will be shared in the next book. I had confided in him, so he was aware of the situation and of how much pain and anguish I was in.

"Leather," his nickname for me, "Leather where you at?"

Through a fit of tears and uncontrolled rage, I responded, "I'm in the parking lot of the Jefferson County Juvenile Courthouse."

"Oh yeah, how did it go?" he asked

I screamed, "They won't even let me in. I have been married to that MF for 18 years; everything that happens in there affects me and my kids and I can't go in? I'm about to kill them both as soon as they come out of this building. I'm going to kill their asses."

"Leather, come over here let me talk to you," he said. "Come on now."

I started driving in the direction of his house but somehow, I lost my way. I was so blind with wrath, I could not find my way to a house I had gone to hundreds of times and had even lived there before. The tears fell so full and rapidly that I couldn't see where I was going. Finally, I stopped my car on the side of the road and realized my son's father was still on the phone.

"Leather, are you coming?" he asked.

"Yeah, I'm coming," I replied

I eventually made it to his house. We sat on the front porch and talked for a while. He reminded me of my decision to stay in my marriage and work things out.

"Your husband is a good man. You told me that you weren't going to hurt that man. You knew this day was coming. Now get yo-self together and stop that crying and acting crazy. It's gone be alright."

He was right, but I was not feeling it at all. I knew it was not the end of the world, but it felt like it.

Every emotion was a tender spot. With pain so intense, I nearly slipped into a depression. I was fatigued all the time. My throat always felt like there was a lump in it and when I tried to talk, my voice came out low and monitored. I was afraid that if I spoke up, I would erupt like a volcano. Whatever words or thoughts that I sought to release struggled to reach the surface. Every syllable had to fight its way through vines and snakeweed that had entangled and weaved themselves around the core of my mind. I found myself crying throughout the day and all night long until there was nothing left.

I couldn't concentrate on anything. I would sit lost in thought. My mind bounced from one negative thought to the next. I was so embarrassed. I needed someone to talk to but usually, I am the go-to person in my circle. So now, who do I open up to? I was a mess.

Pain didn't just materialize in mental anguish; my body also felt the brunt of his betrayal. I can't prove it, but I believe that most diseases are derived from **Dis-Ease**, dis-ease in our spirit and soul causes disease and illness to manifest in our bodies. I was hurting bad, y'all. Every organ, blood vessel, and bodily function ached. The trauma and grief manifested themselves in the diagnosis of five different physical illnesses: Graves' disease, depression, high blood pressure, rheumatoid arthritis, and acid reflux were the byproducts of the grief I was experiencing. Pain and anger were literally killing me. I was struggling but one thing for certain and two things for sure: I did not want to be sick, and I did not want to die. Moreover, lingering and unattended hurt has the potential to morph into self-pity and I didn't want that either.

Hurt is rooted in disappointment. Yes, there is always room for improvement and there is nothing wrong with wanting others to be and do better; however, trusting and expecting people to be no more and no less than what they have proven themselves to be is a surefire way to avoid disappointment. This statement is not to insinuate that people cannot change or that we should settle for less and give up on them. It does offer a way to avoid damaging our emotions and disrupting our peace. It's never the person who disappoints us. It is our unrealized expectations of that person that disappoints us.

Phase 4: Mad as Hell

Mad: Very angry, mentally ill, or insane.

I have heard the phrase **mad as hell** a few times in my life. Anger can present itself in various ways. It can be explosive and violent, or it can be seething and conniving. Either way, unchecked anger has the potential to be destructive and sometimes deadly.

Watching true crime shows is one of my guilty pleasures. There are countless men and women incarcerated because their anger went unchecked. In some cases, they injured or even took someone's life. I find myself asking the same question after every episode. *Did they think they would get away with it? How did they think it would end?*

There was one lady who ran her car over her husband several times after catching him at a hotel with his mistress. She had their daughter in the car with her. It is easy to act without thinking, but there are others, mostly children, to consider. If anger leads to violence, you will face consequences and be held accountable. So, count the cost.

The court bailiff didn't know it, but he had verbalized my feelings in a nutshell. Nearly 20 years of commitment and devotion

did not matter. Almost 20 years of my time, 20 years of sharing my body, mind, and soul didn't matter; 20 years of my love did not matter.

On the outside, we looked like the perfect young family. We attended church every Sunday morning and Wednesday night. We both were committed volunteers in the church. I led a ministry of over two hundred people and taught weekly bible classes. I had not had a drink, used profanity, or even listened to secular music in over fifteen years. I was not perfect, but I had been a good wife and committed to a holy way of life and to my family. As a good church-going woman, I was nothing, if not loyal. But like the court bailiff so forcefully stated, none of that mattered.

By this time, I had put my Christianity on the back burner. Imagine, teaching Christian principles like love and forgiveness at a time when all I could think about was the turmoil that was constantly bombarding my mind and body day in and day out. I wanted to hurt somebody. I wanted to make them suffer just like I was suffering. Eventually, I accepted the fact that I was not in any condition to minister to God's people, so I stepped away from ministry.

My husband was determined to do all he could to save our marriage and I could give less than a damn. He set up marriage counseling at the church, but I was hearing none of it. It is often the position of the church and church folk that we should attack everything in faith. To me, that sounded insensitive. To my ears, this approach sometimes sounds like the woman is to blame for allowing herself to feel and express her pain and that the onus was on me to get over this situation as soon as possible. I felt that the expectation was for me to remain Godly and forgive instantly. I was expected to be strong and pray my way through.

After all, what would Jesus do?

How was I supposed to do that when I was struggling to take a deep breath?

Pray for me, pray for him, pray for us -- damn that! *Where's my butcher knife?*

It pissed me off when folk would quote the Bible to me. Irritated, I thought, "Don't tell me what the Bible says. I teach it on a regular basis, and I can finish your sentences." NO!! After a while, I said it out loud and meant it.

One day we went to a counseling session at our church, and I cut up. I was so indignant. I said to the counselor, "I don't need no damned counseling. I didn't do anything. Why do I need to forgive or do anything else to fix this mess? I didn't get an orgasm, not even a kiss out of the deal," and walked out. Let me remind you this person was my ministry leader. I felt like God already knew where

I was, so putting on a holy show and faking the funk was not going to happen.

What I wanted to do at that moment was heat up a cast-iron skillet and bust that MF right on the top of his forehead. I didn't want to pray. I didn't want to believe. I didn't want to confess the word or meditate. I had a right to be mad and irrational. This plethora of emotions was mine, and I was holding onto it. All I wanted was revenge. *What I really wanted was to cut this joker's body part off with a rusty butcher knife and watch gangrene slowly consume his body.*

I believe that one of the problems in the church, as it relates to challenges and the human experience, is that we don't make room for people to feel or express their feelings. We don't give them a chance to locate and process their emotions. People say stuff like *hold on to God's unchanging hand. You take one step, God will take two,* and all of the other religious phrases we spout when we don't know what else to say.

"So, what exactly does that mean anyway?"

First, I agree that God is a healer, a deliverer, and He will restore me and give me peace. But at that moment I was hurt, confused, and mad as hell.

Experiences like this can be devastating and hurt like hell. However, one thing is guaranteed: **this too shall pass.**

Secondly, you are not to blame. Whatever your man has done was his decision and it had nothing to do with you. I concluded that trying to figure out the why is an exhaustive waste of time. It does not matter. My husband cheated. He shared his body, his mind, and his time with another woman and now they have a child together. That is all I needed to know. Now the question is "What now?"

Never apply a permanent solution to a temporary problem.

Phase 5: I Don't Give a Damn!

Reckless: Lack of restraint, without thinking or caring about the consequences of an action.

One of my sons is a Marine Corp veteran. Deployed to the Middle East in the heat of the Iraqi war, he experienced violence that I cannot even imagine. Bombings, gunfights, IAD, and grenade attacks were a daily occurrence. But the mode of attack that is most interesting to me is the suicide bombings. Everyone is affected by the act, including the bomber, who is affected the most. Reckless behavior is guaranteed to hurt you the most. The suicide bomber is an extreme example but if you spit out of a car window at eighty miles an hour, you will more than likely experience some blowback. Yes, you end up spitting in your own face.

Rage is irrational but it made me feel strong and in control. In a strange way, it made me feel powerful and that power felt good. I was boiling over and liking every bit of it. In other words, I was free to act as indecent as I wanted! AND I DID JUST THAT.

It was here that I discovered a wickedness in me that I did not know existed. It was as if I was a different person. After more than twenty years of no drinking, smoking, cussing or anything else that resembled fleshly sin, I had reached a point where I did not care. With reckless disregard, I began to do and say just about anything and everything that I was big and bad enough to do. It seemed as though a switch flipped in my mind. The person I was becoming had been lurking in the corners of my being, waiting to be unleashed. This alternate personality was ready, willing, and able to wreak havoc on anybody unfortunate enough to offend me, real or imagined. Because I didn't trust anybody, I inadvertently sabotaged many relationships. Most of those lost relationships were with acquaintances. Many of my close relationships suffered damage as well. By this time, the **IT** was no longer a secret. The people who were truly close to me understood that I was struggling and the person they were dealing with at the time was not the person they knew and loved.

My children were taken aback. They no longer recognized me, and I no longer recognized myself. I went all in, y'all. I'm sure it was scary to them. Friends and acquaintances showed their concern by trying to reason with me. I can't tell you the amount of phone calls and free lunches I received. The look on some of their faces when realizing that I had indeed used profanity in our conversation was priceless.

Up until this point, I had been disconnected and detached from the reality of my situation. But now I was fully engaged and ready for all the smoke. Nothing could appease the chaos that had taken over my mind. The anger and rage became part of me, like a second skin. I owned it and no one was going to talk me into letting it go, not ever. I fumed at the suggestion that I was being unfair. I refused to tolerate anyone telling me to forgive -- to let it go. That was the last thing on my mind. I wanted revenge. I wanted a fight and one day out of the blue, I had my chance.

About three years in, I had decided that I was going to get alcohol. So, after dropping off my son at work, I found myself on the way to the liquor store. Now I had not drank in over 20 years, so I was getting Hennessy, my drink of choice from back in the day. My mind was set: *I'm going to get in a quiet corner and drink some cognac; I won't bother anybody, and I don't want anyone to bother me.*

Up to this point, I had not had a conversation with this other woman, nor did I have a desire to. I didn't know her. She didn't owe me anything. As far as I was concerned, she was a non-factor to me. Although I had met her once, I still would not have recognized her on the street. My brain just would not download her image into my mind. After all was said and done, it was my husband with whom I had made a covenant.

While in the shopping center, I happen to see the little boy walking past my car. Because we had met a couple of times before, he recognized me and waved. I waved back. Although I had blocked her face from my memory, I knew the woman with him had to be his mom. Initially, I was not even thinking about confronting her. I dropped my son off at work and proceeded out of the parking lot to get my cocktails. That's when it happened. A switch flipped on and like a volcano, I was ready to erupt and spew lava on whatever and whoever got in the way. I flipped a U-turn thinking to myself, "Oh yeah, it's about that time."

The first time I followed her into the store, I could not find her. "Now I know she is in here," I told myself out loud. My mind was made up. I was not sure what I hoped to achieve by confronting her, but I was determined. This was happening today. Everything in me wanted her to be antagonistic. I was aching for her to say something smart, anything that would give me a reason to punch her in the throat, but I didn't want to traumatize the child. He was innocent but this was going down that day.

I found her. There she was in the children's section. She must have known that I was there for a fight. I don't know what she saw but I know what I felt. Quickly approaching her, I went straight in.

"Hey, I want to talk to you. Now I'm telling you, if you get smart with me, I am going to bust you in your mouth with this cell phone. Are we clear?"

As she riffled through clothes on the rack, I could see her hands shaking. Looking kind of off to the side, her first words to me were, "I wondered why you never said anything to me before now."

Trying to provoke her, I responded, "For what? You ain't shit to me."

The next words from her mouth were, "I'm sorry. I'm married now and I understand how you feel."

I'm not sure if that information was meant to pacify or assure me that the relationship was over or her way of bragging, but it didn't matter. That apology did not phase me one bit. I was furious and wanted a reason to physically attack her. She began to explain her position, talk about her shame, and how she had asked God to forgive her.

"I don't want to hear that. That's not why I'm here. I have two questions for you. How long had you been seeing my husband? And did you know he was married?"

The answers I got sent me into a tailspin.

Yes, she knew he was married, and they had been seeing each other on and off for several years.

SEVERAL YEARS?!?! What the hell?

By the end of our conversation, I accepted the fact that she was not going to give me a reason to thump her in the throat. So, I left her with these words: "Now that you are married, you will reap the harvest from this seed you have sown. Maybe you will be able to bear it."

This encounter did nothing to help me in the way of healing. It pulled me in one direction and one direction only: pure unchecked rage. My downward spiral accelerated. The anger in me boiled over and erupted into full-blown fury.

How could he? Why did he?

I went home and confronted him with the information I had just gathered. I drilled him with one question after another.

Where did you meet?

When did you see her?

Did she cook for you?

Does she wear matching underwear?

Did she make you feel like a man?

He didn't't want to talk about it. His responses were short and without substance. I'm sure he thought he was minimizing my pain by not telling the truth, the whole truth, and nothing but the truth. At the time, his lack of transparency infuriated me. I wanted answers or so I thought. In hindsight, he was probably right. All those detailed nuisances only gave me more mental images to get out of my head.

The discussion morphed into a heated exchange and ended with my husband up against the door with a butcher knife to his chest. There was no way we could sleep in the same house.

"You got to leave here," I screamed. "You can't stay here because I am going to kill you in your sleep."

With both hands up as if to surrender, he agreed. He had to leave that day, or I was going to hurt him. PERIOD!

For the next several months, he would come by the house once a week to leave his paycheck on the dining room table. I spent this time in a haze of confusion. The people in our tribe who had survived my wrath chose not to take sides and I appreciated that. You never really know what people are thinking behind the scenes, but on the surface, they were gracious.

I was the benefactor of plenty of free meals. One evening my sister-in-law invited me to dinner so that we could talk. This was one of the most transparent conversations I had about the situation, and it turned out to be a pivotal point on my road to recovery. During this conversation, it became apparent that there would be no coddling and no sidestepping. Transparency and honesty were the themes of the day.

Yes, I was hurt. Yes, I was angry. And although I had every right to be, I also had a choice as to whether I would remain that way. This conversation was not about us as a couple. We would not be discussing him, her, or the child they had created together. This conversation was not even about my children or whether I would stay with my husband or tell him to kick rocks. This talk would be all about me. It was about me being accountable to myself.

How did I want to show up in the room? What type of aura did I want to envelop the spaces I occupied? She reminded me of the fact that nobody is responsible for my happiness and peace of mind except for me. It was time to decide...

What did I want?

Who did I want to be?

How did I want to live the rest of my life?

I admitted that I was exhausted. Disappointment and hurt, anger and rage had nearly drained the life out of me. It was to the point that I didn't recognize or like the person in the mirror. Negativity had blinded me. I was still suffocating and all I could see was darkness. At that point, all I wanted was to breathe.

The Red Tag Syndrome

The act of devaluing or cheapening one's own self-worth in order to exact revenge on someone who betrayed you.

The Bible tells the story of the Prodigal Son who asked for and received his inheritance. As the story goes, he went away and spent all he had on riotous living. Of the many priceless nuggets in this story, one little-discussed lesson centers around him getting a revelation of who he really was. According to the text, although he longed to eat from the "husk that the swine ate," no account says that he did so. He came to himself before stooping that low.

Sexual promiscuity was never in my DNA. But it was easy to justify in this case. If he did it, I am going to do it too, but I was never a cheater. Full disclosure -- I came close but that is not how I get down. I was reckless but that is the one thing that I could not bring myself to do. I am not common or cheap and this situation was not going to put me on the clearance aisle.

Notes:

Notes:

Notes:

The Recovery, Restoration, and Discovery

Exploring The "How To"

"Don't Wait for The Storm to Pass...Learn How to Dance in The Rain." - Let Me Breathe

Agonizing over a situation this intensely for this long was out of character for me. My general personality is to bounce back.

I have always been a "hot water cornbread" or "use what I got to get what I want" kind of person. Normally, I don't spend too much time on woulda, coulda, shouldas, or worrying about what I don't have or what didn't go right. I'm more like, *Let's assess where we are, inventory what we have, and move on towards a solution with what we have.*

Many women's existence is fueled by hurt, anger, and bitterness. They allow offenses to mold their worldview and dictate the way they show up in the world. For these sisters, misery is a never-ending state of being. She is the type of person who can always locate the problem in every situation but seldom arrives at the table with a solution. She secretly, or not so secretly, rejoices when others suffer. If you ask her what she wants, she can only articulate what she does not want. She is the chick who can't take yes for an answer and believes that a good thing is too good to be true. You know her, the stink-face chick that I mentioned earlier.

Metaphorically, I was in a deep, dark hole suffering from a gut punch and a thump to the throat. For nearly six years, I was an emotional wreck, crouched in a corner, licking my wounds and sulking about the wrong done to me. I had taken the posture of a victim. I was exhausted and sick and tired of being sick and tired.

I have one shot at this life and showing up as the stink-face chick is not cute AT ALL. So, I had a choice to make. I could stay in the gloomy abyss of despair, or I could stand upright, put my dukes up and fight. What I discovered is there is a difference between living and existing. I wanted to live. I wanted to be happy. I needed to be free. As I stated earlier, I am a do-or-die kind of person, so for me, the decision to fight for my life was the only choice.

Let the brawl begin… I am worth the fight.

"Happiness is a journey, not a destination."

- Alfred D Souza

Recovery

The action or process of regaining possession or control of something taken or lost.

On a practical level, the process of recovery can be as intense and unnerving as the initial pain. Before I could reconstruct my life, I first had to tear down some things inside of me. Dealing with my own weaknesses and imperfections was tough. This exercise was like scraping the bottom of a burnt pot. You scrape off a little at a time, let it sit, and start again later until the soot is gone. When you finish, the results are very satisfying, and you are happy you did.

One of my pet peeves is when people are encouraged to do something without having a blueprint or some instruction on achieving said desire. Vague or ambiguous instruction only breeds frustration and confusion. People often get frustrated and end up more despondent than they were initially.

I will not lie to you. This journey to freedom is hard. Sometimes it can feel lonely. And although resources were available to me, they proved to be inadequate. Resources available through the church were well-meaning and sincere but were not sound on structure, and I somehow felt stifled by the expectation to do the right thing, the Godly thing. This expectation, real or perceived, bothered me greatly. If I was feeling indignant and disrespectful during a session, I wanted to be able to express those emotions. I did not feel free to do that. This could have been all in my head but nonetheless, that is how I felt. Resources in the secular community provided structure and a safe place for freedom of expression but very little in the way of tending to my spiritual wellbeing. I am still a child of God and Christianity is the core of my belief system. Conversely, if I had resolved to lift my voice to bind the enemy and war in the spirit for a minute, I wanted the freedom to do that as well.

I realized that I needed more than a cheerleader, some encouraging words, or a place to lash out. What I needed were specific instructions and tools to help me. What I needed was a game plan to get out of the deep dark hole I was in.

It took a long time for me to heal. If you have experienced a similar betrayal or are struggling with any type of emotional trauma, it is my hope that you find something on the pages of this book that helps you to succeed on your journey to wholeness.

"The Journey of a Thousand Miles Begins with a Single Step." - Lao Tzo

The information in this section is simply me sharing what worked for me. Take what you need to help you emerge from your traumatic experience better and not bitter.

Decide

To select a definite course of action. The Latin root word means to cut of or eliminate any other options.

During the Spanish Conquest, military leader Henan Cortes ordered his men to burn the boats they had used to bring them to the shores of Mexico. This act indicated a definite decision to cut away or destroy any option to retreat from the battle.

Without a firm decision, moving forward would have been impossible. Deciding comes first and is the most important step. This was half the battle.

Up until this point in my life, I am not sure if I had ever thought of myself as a priority. Consequently, the question of "what I wanted" was problematic on its own. I first had to embrace the fact that I had a right to choose what I wanted and how I wanted it. Furthermore, I did not need to justify my decision or my desire to anyone.

Discovering the answer to that question in a real and honest way was a huge part of my process. Initially, I had no idea what I wanted. You may be feeling the same way but let me encourage you, Sis. It is okay. It will come to you.

I spent several years consumed by confusion and frustration. It was easy for me to articulate what I didn't want. I was certain of one thing; I did not want to live the rest of my life as a Mad Black Woman.

I had to consider: How much more of me was I willing to give away? How much more of my life would I allow this situation to suffocate? The answer to those questions was a resounding **zero**. The bad "juju" was killing me, spiritually, mentally, and physically. I am much too cute for that...

"Adjust Your Crown and Pull Yourself Together."

Restoration

The act of restoring to a better, higher, or more worthy state.

The house fire I mentioned earlier was alarming. My initial response was despair. All of our belongings were damaged or destroyed by either fire, water, smoke or all three. It was all gone. However, after some time, planning, and a lot of hard work, the restorations were complete. As a result, the house looked better and was more functional than it had been before the fire. Just like my house, the process of restoration made me better spiritually, mentally, and physically.

Forgive Him

I already know what you're thinking. Trust me, this is imperative. Forgiveness and restoration are two different things. I'm not suggesting that you let him back into your life or suppress your feelings and act as if it is all good. I'm talking about making a choice to **let it go**. This is not to say that you are going to feel forgiveness when you do this. You have simply made a choice.

You may wonder how did I do this? Open your mouth and say out of it, "1 forgive JIM BOB for what he has done to me." PERIOD. Let that simmer for a minute. This can feel extremely awkward. You may even think that nothing is happening. You may be experiencing the exact same hurt you did the week before you said it. That's okay. Give your feelings time to catch up with your decision. You may have to do this more than a few times. Every time those negative feelings of anger and unforgiveness start to creep up, open your mouth and say it again. Even through the tears and emotional fits, open your mouth and confirm that forgiveness in this case is a settled issue.

Forgive Yourself

I had to learn to forgive myself. Admittedly, there were red flags that I either missed, dismissed, or completely ignored.

How could I have been so stupid?

But when I think about it, what could I have done to prevent it? I could have confronted him, followed him, or checked his phone; none of that would have made any difference. I can't make a grown man behave. He was going to do what he wanted to do. No ma'am! Jealousy has never been my thing. I did nothing to deserve this. His choices had nothing to do with me. So, I forgave myself and accepted that this was not my fault. I had to forgive him, not because he deserved my forgiveness, but because I deserved peace.

Practicing the art of meditation helped me to put things in perspective. It is amazing what a few consistent moments of silence can do for the soul.

Verbal faith confessions and self-affirmations helped me embrace my truth. I finally realized that I had nothing to feel awkward, self-conscious, or ashamed about. This man decided and followed up on it. His actions do not affect my personal worth and value at all. There is not a thing wrong with me. I don't have to prove myself to him and no one else. I am enough just as I am. PERIOD!

Whenever I speak about this part, powerful, beautiful, accomplished women come to mind. Women like Hillary Clinton, Mary J. Blige, and the baddest chick in the game, Beyonce -- all experienced the pain of infidelity. These women were not even afforded the benefit of privacy. Can you imagine being Mrs. Knowles Carter herself going through this trauma with the whole world watching? Oh girl, you have got to know your worth to grind this out without spazzing all the way out. Give yourself a break.

" Learn to dance in the storm."

Discovery

The act or process of seeing, finding, or realizing something.

On your way to self-discovery, you will realize that emotions are tricky and inconsistent. One minute you feel totally in control and the next minute you feel helpless and weak. Your feelings are real, and it is important to understand what you are up against. Identifying specific emotions can feel a little awkward but being clearer on what you are experiencing will help you to plot an adequate defense and execute an effective offense.

Do Something Just for You

Suddenly, you look in the mirror and realize that you don't know the woman looking back at you. Notice, I didn't say *recognize her*. I said you don't **know her**. To recognize her would indicate that you are familiar and have, at some point, known that woman looking back at you. The truth is a lot of us have never known her. The woman looking back at you is a stranger, busy wearing labels and being everything to everybody. I had never made time to get to know me as a woman or as a person. I never took the time to be good to me. I didn't even know my favorite color was orange until I was in my early forties. That sounds simple but it's sad.

It's funny how the mundane trappings of existence can conceal and snuff out the real you. One of my best friends is a doctor. Achieving a goal like this one is a challenge, to say the least, not to mention being a Black woman in such a high-pressure, male-dominated field. That part is a struggle alone. This sister earned her medical license as a single mother with very little support from others. She then moved to another state where she did not know a soul, carved out a life for her and her children, and is now succeeding on a level that she admits she had always dreamed of as a little girl. During one of our many conversations, she shared what I thought was a profound and yet troubling statement. One day while talking about this book and its impact, I noticed that she kind of trailed off. Turning her gaze towards me she said, "You know I have never celebrated myself." She said, "I am in my fifties, and I have never taken the time to celebrate me." The process of discovery will reveal truths like this one.

Recovering from the pain of my husband's infidelity forced me to deal with me. Honey, that sounds simple, but it is not! This reckoning is uncomfortable. It is rough, messy, and hurts like hell to pull the scabs off. But it is necessary and sets the stage for the beginning of inner healing and restoration.

As I mentioned before, during the heat of my recovery, I was introduced to the discipline of mindful meditation. This changed my entire life. It was through mindfulness and meditation that I discovered some interesting characteristics that I had never considered before. For example, my tendency to over-commit stems from a desire to prove that I am a nice person. However, because of this flaw, I sometimes come off as flaky and undependable. That is not how I want to present. The solution was to learn to say "no" and accept my own limitations.

Another flaw has to do with an annoying tendency to try and fix everybody's problem or my knack for offering unsolicited advice to people. Sometimes others don't want any input; they just want a listening ear. I tended to overstep boundaries by trying to offer a solution for their issue. Now my position is to be a support and a listening ear. I try to offer advice only when asked. I have not reached perfection, however, I am doing much better. I choose to celebrate the small victories.

Take time to think about what turns you on. What are some of the things you have always wanted to do that you placed way in the back of your mind? I had always wanted a college degree, so I enrolled in school and earned associate's and bachelor's degrees. This move served me in more than one way. I achieved a lifelong goal that helped to take my mind off what had happened and gave me a reason to be proud of myself. You don't have to go that deep. You may want to learn to swim, take up knitting, or gardening. Whatever you find to put your hands on, do you.

"Celebrate You No Matter How Small the Victory."

Take Your Time, Sis

Unfortunately, women wear the cloak of fixer in the home, in the community, and especially in church. During the thick of my recovery, I felt that the onus was on me to hurry up and get over this thing. My perception of the messages I was getting from my faith community left me believing that I was taking too long, therefore, my faith in God and the level of my Christianity were in question.

My feelings, mood, and emotions were all over the place. I was suffering from humiliation, mental anguish, and embarrassment along with a host of other negative emotions, which were nearly unbearable. My mental state was affecting my physical health, and my ability to think clearly, and because I am a business owner, my ability to make money weakened. There was no way I could rush through that. Don't allow others to place unrealistic demands on you. This is your journey; go at your own pace, but you must keep moving forward. I was hurt and confused. I WAS NOT CRAZY, and neither are you.

You are in survival mode and need all your energy to do what needs to be done to be free from anguish. Be careful not to overwhelm yourself. This can take you to the other end of the spectrum and cause a bigger mess.

"Honesty has a power that very few people can handle."

Keep Your Tribe Small

Keeping your circle tight is a protection mechanism. Too many voices will only serve to increase your confusion.

I cannot express how important this is. You need an honest voice of reason in your corner. I am grateful to my sister-in-law for being that voice for me. She gave it to me straight, no chaser. I needed to be shocked back into reality. This may not be true for everyone but for me, the environment of *I don't give a hoot* was becoming my reality. Mean and brash was the way. I had become sour and uncaring. For a moment, it felt good. This gave me surges of what I call faux-strength. Yes, I made that one up. What I was experiencing was a pseudo kind of strength. It was all a temporary façade. I was turning into the stink face chick and didn't even know it.

Be sure that the people with whom you confide in and those whom you allow to pour into you are honest with you. What you do not need are "yes" folk or somebody who is struggling with similar issues of their own.

Be Quiet

Peace is priceless. Mindful meditation has proven to be a game changer for me and many others in the pursuit of wholeness and peace. A simple deep breathing exercise will help you to calm down when negative emotions attempt to take over and dictate your actions.

A few minutes of silence on a regular basis helped me to put things in perspective and recognize the triggers that threatened to send me spiraling out of control again. I began with some guided meditation from YouTube. Listed below are a few of many to choose from. These are the ones that worked for me. I encourage you to do your own research to find an appropriate fit for you.

- Guided Meditations by Lavendaire
- Guided Meditations by Dr. Wayne Dyer
- Guided Meditations by Bob Proctor

Speak On It!

Your words have power. If you intend to take back your joy and peace, this part is vital. You and only you have the ability to speak life and death into your situation. This is not to suggest that you lie or be in denial. For instance, instead of saying you are depressed, you may say, "I believe I have joy." If this is currently a challenge for you, at least do not refer to yourself or your situation in a negative light. To do so is counterproductive to your efforts to heal.

When there is no one else to encourage us, we have to encourage ourselves. Below is a list of faith confessions or affirmations that I continue to use to this day. This exercise helps me to embrace and appreciate my own personal value and self-worth. Recite these to yourself consistently until they become second nature. Feel free to use these. You may want to add your own personal confessions.

- I am enough as I am
- I am loved
- I am protected
- My mind is at peace
- I will live and not die
- I am whole in my spirit, soul and body
- I am beautiful inside and out

- Nothing can stop me
- My joy overflows
- Three things I love about me are _____

Putting In the Work

To put in the work implies action, movement, or activity in pursuit of achieving a desired goal. It has been said that anything worth having is worth working for. Your journey to better requires action. You have to do something.

Journaling

There are so many benefits to participating in this exercise. Writing is therapeutic and a vehicle of release. Journaling is a wonderful outlet and safe space for purging your thoughts and communicating your truth without inhibition. You can be as real as you want to be here Sis. I recommend that you hold nothing back. Journaling can also be your creative space -- the place where you can develop components of your vision for your future. Start by asking yourself this series of questions.

How has this experience impacted...

- Key areas of my life?
- My spiritual life?
- Relationship with children, family, and friends?
- Work/business?
- My physical health?
- My mental health?

Self-Care Is Not Selfishness. It Is a Must!

Don't believe the hype. You are not selfish. You are in survival mode and need to make time for self-care. Emotional self-care helps us to look inward and identify our emotional needs and what it takes to fulfill those needs. As you consistently practice self-awareness and exercise the skills necessary to manage your emotions, you learn self-compassion or the act of being kind to yourself. It is hard to be every woman when you are running on fumes. Be purposeful in pursuing your recovery. It is not enough to talk about healing and restoration. You must now mix action with your faith, hope, or expectation and do something. Your *something* could be a daily walk in the park or visiting the local museum. Whatever brings you a bit of peace, do it.

Below are a few ideas that may appeal to you as you make yourself a priority.

Action Items

1. Develop a relaxing evening ritual
2. Get a therapist
3. Try some mindful exercises to help bring you into the present moment
4. Try some adult coloring as a form of anxiety and/or stress release
5. Remind yourself of the good stuff in life by writing a list of things you're grateful to have
6. Do some stretching exercises
7. Take a walk in the park
8. Drink more water
9. Attend exercise classes or find some YouTube exercise videos.
10. Get a massage
11. Go out and spend 10 minutes under the sun
12. Go for a bike ride to nowhere in particular
13. Go hiking, camping, or backpacking and spend some time in nature
14. Find an old sitcom and laugh

15. Learn to swim
16. Write a love letter to the girl in the mirror
17. Start a 10-Day Journal (daily thoughts)
18. Start a 30-Day Gratitude Journal
19. Think of five things you have to be thankful for each day. It's okay if you repeat it from time to time
20. Complete the worksheets provided as an accompaniment to this book

For some of us, these activities will be a challenge. Do not be hard on yourself. The goal is progress, not perfection. Go at your own pace, but do not quit. Do not give up on you. You are worth the fight.

The Epilogue
So Now What?

My traumatic journey started because of my husband's infidelity. However, disappointment can be caused by any number of things and/or people in your life. It doesn't have to be a marriage or intimate relationship. Some of us struggle with our children, parents, siblings, or other family drama. Feeling devalued, ignored, lied to, and taken for granted can be painful no matter the source. Some are disappointed in themselves and have regret over careers and other life choices or for doing or not doing something that may or may not be in their control. Some have lost loved ones and have never learned, nor had the time, to process it. All these situations can send us spiraling out of control or paralyze and hinder our progress. My journey to wholeness began over fifteen years ago. It took me six years to break free from the negative vibes that were attempting to devour me.

Change is inevitable. And this experience was definitely life-changing for me. It is up to us to determine what impact that change would have on my life.

This book is my attempt to use my life experiences to help other women to recover from emotional wounds, but you must do the work. It is my hope that the strategies, principles, and suggestions outlined in this book will help you in your journey to wholeness. It is my prayer that you apply what you have learned here to any situation that is holding you hostage.

Will you show up as the shining star, the beautiful gorgeous being that you are, or will you be the stink face chick?

Today my husband and I are going stronger than ever. We are now better friends than ever before, and our relationship is better than it has ever been. We like, love, and respect each other, and I am secure in my marriage. I can stand and declare that I am happy and more fulfilled than I have ever been in my adult life.

I don't know if reconciliation will be your path. As it relates to the restoration of your marriage and other love relationships, you do what it takes for you to be free. You get one chance at this life; my hope is that you live it better and not bitter

Choose life so you can breathe again.

You Have Got to Discover YOU, What You Do, and Trust It!

Barbra Streisand

Notes:

Notes:

Notes:

Notes:

About Angela Williams

Angela C. Williams is a wife, mother, award-winning speaker, realtor youth advocate, founder of #POPOFF, "A Summit 4 Youth by Youth" and the owner of Activate Emotional Intelligence Academy. She is also the author of "He Cheated! So, What Now?" and founder of the So What Now Conference. With a degree in Communications/ Public Relations and Sociology, she has spent the last several years encouraging wounded women and teens to love, believe, and trust themselves while embracing all of life's possibilities.

Growing up in a single-family home on the south side of Birmingham, Alabama during the 70s and 80s forced her to mature quickly. Coming of age in such a challenging experience taught her the value of perseverance, self-confidence, and self-reliance.

Angela is an ordinary woman. Just like several other ordinary women, she has been betrayed by the act of infidelity. He Cheated! So, What Now? shares her six-year journey to wholeness, along with tools and strategies she used to overcome very painful circumstances and walk in peace. This book is designed to help you navigate in less time than it took her to emerge from pain and disappointment better not bitter.

www.ingramcontent.com/pod-product-compliance
Lightning Source LLC
Chambersburg PA
CBHW030044100526
44590CB00011B/324